Customer Service Tips: *How to Improve Customer Service* Part 3 of a Series

by

Rosanne D'Ausilio, PhD
Customer Service Expert

Published in the United States by
Champion for the Human Press

ISBN# -0-9772360-5-6

Introduction

The preamble to the US Constitution begins, "we, the people..." I believe we, the people, are who make the difference.

I am not trying to impress you, but impress upon you, the impact you and your people have not only on the customer, internal and external, current or potential, but the bottom line as well.

The interaction anyone has at any level with your employees, including you, gives any customer an opportunity to make a judgment about you, your company, all companies like yours.

70-90% of what happens with customers is driven by human nature, having nothing to do with technology. Qualities found in human interaction can eliminate much of the frustration leading to unnecessary escalations. Sometimes a customer wants interaction—not automation.

I often talk about taking customer service and 'kicking it up a notch.' In the food industry, the word 'lagniappe' is often used. Its definition is "a small present given to a customer with a purchase. For example, when you go to the bakery and buy a dozen donuts or bagels, you oftentimes get a 'free' one or a baker's dozen.

That's what customer service should be about--giving the customer more than they expected.

Here is a working definition so we're all on the same page.

Customer service is 'those activities provided by a company's employees that enhance the ability of a customer to realize the full potential value of a product or service before and after the sale is made, thereby leading to satisfaction and repurchase.'

Index

How to Use This Book

There are several ways to get the most out of this book:

1. Refer to the Index and choose the topics that interest you, or are plaguing you

2. Read the tips from 47 through 77 (from beginning to end of the book)

3. Open the book at random and read wherever your eyes take you – probably wherever your eyes land is something you need or want to pay attention to

And then:

Implement the suggestions, recommendations, and techniques.

Share what impacted you with friends, family, co-workers.

Positively impact your personal and professional life.

My goal is that you not only enjoy the book, but most importantly, add value to your life both personally and professionally.

It's not necessary that you read Part I or Part 2 of this Series to get value out of Part 3. Of course, these are available to you should you so desire.

Tip #47

Great Calls

I'm sure you all have stories of great calls, the ones that made your day. Everything went perfectly from the very beginning. You and the customer were on the same wave length. Perhaps you had a humorous exchange. Your listening was acute, and your response was right on. You really helped the customer. He/she thanked you profusely for doing such a good job, for taking such great care of them. You felt great. You knew, even before they said so, that you had done a great job.

Can you remember having that feeling? Can you recreate it right now? Are you smiling just thinking about it? Ask yourself these 3 questions?

1) What was different about that call?

What was different about the call was not the customer. The common denominator in all your calls is not the customer, but you, yourself, the person sitting in your chair. You were right there with the customer, listening attentively, and responding accordingly. Your attitude was positive and it was reflected in the call, and perhaps even acknowledged by you and the customer.

2) How long did that feeling last?

Did you give the feeling away to the next customer? By that I mean, when you are feeling good, you get to choose how long that feeling lasts. You can take it into your next call or you can conveniently forget it, especially if the next customer is the dreaded call from hell. You have a choice here. You can choose to keep the positive feeling with you for the next call, for the next half dozen calls, for the entire day if you like. Or you can assign responsibility for feeling good to the customer, and take no responsibility for your participation in the interaction. When you do this, then when you hang up, the good feelings goes with the customer.

"How important is this?" is a good question to ask yourself. Not only for the upset, but for the good feeling too. You are then at choice as to what to do with the feeling, or where to put it. You can choose to let go of the negative ones (if you so desire) and opt for the good feelings. Again, the good news and the bad news is that you have a choice. Commit to making good choices in your own behalf, one call at a time, one day at a time.

3) How can you recreate the feeling?

A very easy way to remember the conversation is to share it with friends, family, and coworkers. You share all your 'war stories,' don't you? It's just as important to share your 'wins.' It makes them more real for you and reinforces the memory. When a really upsetting call happens, you can remember the good call and neutralize the feelings.

Again, if you have questions, comments, feedback, or topics you'd like covered, please continue to email me at rosanne@HumanTechTips.com.

Tip #48

Metrics

In Tip #38 we listed the metrics effected by training. In this tip, we're going to show you the impact of rubbing three of these metrics together.

First, let's define what we're talking about.

1) Adherence to Schedule - Percentage of time a CSR logs in on time for the start of a shift, returns from breaks promptly, returns from lunch, etc.

2) Occupancy - How often the CSR is actually doing his/her specified job for which they are paid, i.e., in conversation with a customer.

3) Attendance - How often a CSR is absent from work, excluding excused absences like vacations, jury duty, etc.

Hypothetical percentages for a 100 person organization:

75% attendance

82% adherence to schedule

60% occupancy

We begin with

100 people

x75% attendance

75 people are at work

x82% adherence to schedule

61.5 of the people at work are on time

x60% occupancy

36.9 people are doing their job, being productive

And you are paying for how many? Yes, 100, yet only 37 people are being productive! The other 63 are doing something else.

At first glance, you might think these percentages aren't so bad, but when you rub them together, the facts don't lie. Plug in your own numbers and see where you're at. You might be surprised.

At one training we merely brought these numbers to the awareness of the participants and within several days, the stats went up. It could be as simple as someone clocking in, and then going for coffee for 10 minutes. Instead of going for coffee for 10 minutes, and then clocking in.

Next tip I'll tell you what the goal should be for these metrics.

Again, if you have questions, comments, feedback, or topics you'd like covered, please continue to email me at rosanne@HumanTechTips.com.

Tip #49

Goals

Here they are, together with the formula again:

90% Attendance

85% Adherence to Schedule

80% Occupancy

Using our 100 person company:

100 people

x90% attendance

90 people are at work

x85% - adherence to schedule

76.5 of these people are on time

x80% occupancy

61.2 are doing their job, being productive

And again you're paying for how many? 100! But this is still better than the 36.9 with our original example.

The first step is awareness. The more awareness, the more control. If these metrics pose a problem for you, begin instituting small changes to raise awareness first and then levels of performance and productivity.

I've included the definitions below so you don't have to go back to the last tip.

1) Adherence to Schedule - Percentage of time a CSR logs in on time for the start of a shift, returns from breaks promptly, returns from lunch, etc.

2) Occupancy - How often the CSR is actually doing his/her specified job for which they are paid, i.e., in conversation with a customer.

3) Attendance - How often a CSR is absent from work, excluding excused absences like vacations, jury duty, etc.

If you have questions, comments, feedback, or topics you'd like covered, please continue to email me at rosanne@HumanTechTips.com.

Tip #50

Patience

Be patient with your customers. When you hear the same thing over and over again, it's not easy, is it? But it's worth it. Be proactive, make a decision that for the next three calls you am going to be patient with your customers (we mean internal as well as external). Then notice how those interactions went. Ask yourself these questions.

1. Were the calls easier for you to handle?

2. Was the customer surprised?

3. Did they feel taken care of?

4. Did the call close in a timely fashion?

5. How did you feel after those calls?

When I am being patient with a customer (or a spouse, child, mother, father), I feel good about myself and I am not as easy to engage. By that I mean, I can maintain my perspective because I have chosen not to let anyone or anything bother me, but rather, to be patient.

When you easily accomplish three calls, move it to six calls. When you are comfortable with six calls, kick it up a notch to 12 calls.

Before you know it, your stress level has decreased and you are looking forward to your daily challenge of being patient with your customers (people). This is truly a win/win/win situation.

If you have questions, comments, feedback, or topics you'd like covered, please continue to email me at rosanne@HumanTechTips.com.

Tip #51

Conflicts

Speaking in our last tip about win/win situations, it's time to get back to the issue of conflicts, per your survey requests.

Some conflicts are hardly noticeable as they ebb and flow through our daily encounters. Others grow into intense disputes that spawn interpersonal tragedies.* Dan Dana defines three levels of conflict as:

Blips

Clashes

Crisis

The Blip

Blips are inevitable. For most people, few days spent in intensely interdependent interaction with people are entirely free of minor annoyances. However, blips pose no threat to the relationship, nor do they produce disharmony that breaks down teamwork.

For example, suppose a co worker used your coffee cup to water plants in the office and you asked her to use something else, and the next day she was using your coffee cup. If you are otherwise cordial and cooperative, this annoyance probably can be handled by reminding the person of your request or wishes.

However, sometimes reminders don't work and the situation deteriorates. As blips accumulate and tension mounts, communication breaks down, sometimes despite your best efforts.

How do you know when the line between a blip and a clash has been crossed? Indications are:

- Repeated disputes about the same issue, perhaps spread over days or weeks

- Arguing over an increasing number of issues
- Feeling less cooperative toward the other
- Feeling less trusting of the other's sincere good will
- Remaining angry at the other for a longer period, hours or days

You are then headed toward a clash.

The Clash

Clashes threaten the form of the basic relationship, but do not end a relationship.

Here's an example: your co-worker on a team project made a number of mistakes that you had to work overtime to correct. When confronted, he shrugs it off, dismissing your complaints as unimportant. Your resentment grows as you are unable to get him to acknowledge your needs.

In responding to a clash, it's important to avoid some common pitfalls. Hunters in the jungle fight or flee, but this is not applicable here. So don't walk away, hang up, or otherwise terminate contact is a retaliatory tactic.

Nor does it work to use threats, intimidation, or coercion to pressure the other person to comply with your wishes. These are power plays—that is, where one person tries to impose a one-sided solution.

The Crisis

A clash has escalated to a crisis when:

- You have decided to terminate the relationship
- You fear that the other will terminate the relationship
- You sense the relationship is unhealthy, and fear that you are vulnerable to emotional harm by remaining in it

For instance, your manager or direct report rates you 'unsatisfactory' in your latest performance appraisal. Believing the evaluation unfair, you attempt to speak to him/her, only to be told it is a closed issue. Your resentment about not being given an opportunity to rebut the negative appraisal is eroding your loyalty to your employer.

What is needed here are conciliatory gestures which will be discussed in our next tip.

If you have questions, comments, feedback, or topics you'd like covered, please continue to email me at rosanne@HumanTechTips.com.

Tip #52

Conciliatory Gestures

Continuing our conversation on conflict, in our last tip (#51) we listed the 3 levels (Blips, Clash, Crisis). As promised, we're talking today about conciliatory gestures.

If you want to save your job—or your self-respect—a conciliatory gesture is needed. What do we mean by that? A conciliatory gesture is: a behavior that signals a shift in attitude from me-against-you to us-against-the-problem or issue.

Usually the gesture is verbal but it doesn't have to be. Its major purpose is to demonstrate a desire or openness to resolve a conflict in a mutually acceptable way.

All conciliatory gestures feel risky to express, because making them exposes you to further rejection. Even so, no crisis can be resolved satisfactorily without taking that risk.

Some forms of conciliatory gestures are:

- Apologizing
- Expressing regret for one's past behavior
- Conceding on a contested issue
- Offering a compromise
- Expressing empathy
- Recognizing the legitimacy of the other's point of view
- Revealing one's own underlying needs/emotional issues
- Disclosing one's thoughts, feelings, motives, and past history as they pertain to the conflict
- Asking for honest feedback
- Expressing positive feelings for other—affection, admiration, respect
- Accepting personal responsibility for part of the problem

- Initiating a search for both-gain (win/win) solutions

Try them all at least once, and then choose the ones that work for you.

Why? Because what customers really want (what we all want) is:

- Accuracy
- Personalized service
- Customized response
- Promptness in response
- Sensitivity

And as we have said many times,

- To be treated with dignity
- To be treated with respect,
- To be listened to

If you have questions, comments, feedback, or topics you'd like covered, please continue to email me at rosanne@HumanTechTips.com.

Tip #53

Competition

Continuing our conversation on conflict, in the next several tips, we will address the various styles on our way to win/win. Today's style is Competition.

Competition: This is where sarcastic, snide remarks, usually yelled live. 'You never do this right,' 'you always do that.' 'You should have done it this way.' The key words here are 'always, never, should.' This construct is hostile and/or competitive. It is win/lose. One of us is going to win and one of us is going to lose.

We don't want to leave out the people who are competitive with you, who try to manipulate or verbally abuse you. They are using a competitive style and you need a way to get them out of it and into a more productive style. In order to do so, you must take them by surprise. Here's a simple exercise to demonstrate..

Please put your hands together, palm to palm in front of you, chest high (as if you were going to pray). Now I want you to push your right hand against your left hand as hard as you can. At the same time I want you to push your left hand against your right as hard as you can. Harder. Push harder. Okay, stop! What happened? I suggest nothing happened. And how did it feel? Probably frustrating, useless, like you're not getting anywhere? Maybe even somewhat tense?

Did you also notice the harder one hand pushed, the harder the other hand pushed? This is what happens when two people are in conflict, and one person starts out in a competitive style.

When someone comes at you in a competitive style, if you resist, you actually make them stronger. It's like your hands. If you hit back, you strengthen them.

If you want them to lose the wind in their sails, you cannot resist them, you cannot defend yourself, and you cannot counter attack them. As much as you may want to do that in the short run, it will not serve your long range intentions. You need to find a way to get out of their path. When you get out of their path, what happens? They take a fall.

Here are some concrete strategies to use, figuratively, of course. Let me create a scenario. Okay, I work for you and I just turned in a report that is a piece of trash. You gave me 10 days to work on it. You tell me I'm an idiot, I'm incompetent, I can't do anything right, what's wrong with me! Obviously they're yelling and I'm standing there quietly, and then I say in a neutral tone, "Is there anything you want to add before I respond? Now you may go off on me again, once or twice even. Each time, I say in a neutral tone, "Is there anything else you want to add before I respond?'. This is the last thing they expect and usually will say, "well, no."

Now in the short run, I want to rip your face off, but in the long run I want to work with you better. I don't want to be treated like that in the future. So my response is very consistent with my long range intention. How can we work this out in the future?

By the way, this works great even when someone isn't angry. Sometimes in your earnestness to serve, you don't let the other person complete what they need to say. So asking 'is there anything you want to add before I respond?' allows them the courtesy to complete what they want to say.

Next tip we'll discuss the Agreement strategy.

If you have questions, comments, feedback, or topics you'd like covered, please continue to email me at rosanne@HumanTechTips.com.

Tip #54

Agreement

Continuing our conversation on conflict, in the next several tips, we will address the various styles on our way to win/win. Today's style is Agreement.

Agreement: Here you agree with them even more than they would agree with themselves. It's like the good cop/bad cop routine, or one nice guy and one who flies off the handle. You reverse roles and the person calms down. If you take their position, they flip over to yours. For those of you with children, this works great with them.

My favorite example is when a child says, "I hate you, you're the worst mother in the world." If I respond, "Young lady, you don't talk to your mother that way, go to your room," we're both in a competitive style and as we learned in our last tip, no one wins.

However, if I agree with her and say, "I'm the worst mother, are you sure? I'm so excited about this. I have been in this contest for 7 years and until now the best I ever got was runner up. Thank you. Thank you so much." And then I put my arms around her and kiss her. She won't know what hit her. And immediately the conflict is diffused.

Next tip we'll discuss the Rephrase strategy.

If you have questions, comments, feedback, or topics you'd like covered, please continue to email me at rosanne@HumanTechTips.com.

Tip #55

Rephrase

Continuing our conversation on conflict, in the next several tips, we will address the various styles on our way to win/win. Today's style is Rephrase.

Rephrase: Tell the other person basically what they're saying. This is so simple and so effective in the middle of a conflict. It works whether either party know it's being used or not.

Recently I had some very costly car repairs done. Ten minutes after I left the garage, having been assured that the car had been road tested and all was fine, I was putt putting up a hill.

I pulled over and called the station saying, "This is Mrs. D. and I am stuck. I just paid you all this money and here I am stuck. What is wrong with you people!"

When I stopped for a breath, he said, "Wow, Mrs. D., you are really upset." I said, "You bet I'm upset. I count on my car. I have to be places at certain times and you guys didn't fix it right and I paid you all this money."

Again he said, "Wow, you're really upset." At this point I said, "So what are you going to do about it?" He said, "I'll have a tow truck come and get the car. Meanwhile I'm on my way over to look at it myself."

Once my upset was acknowledged, I could move into 'so what are you going to do about it.' If he hadn't acknowledged my upset, I would still be yelling. He had great listening skills. Even though I knew what he was doing, I was moved to a productive solution.

The principle is: Do something that does not resist them and catches them off guard, so you can move to a more productive interaction.

Next tip we'll discuss the Avoidance strategy.

If you have questions, comments, feedback, or topics you'd like covered, please continue to email me at rosanne@HumanTechTips.com

Tip #56

Avoidance

Continuing our conversation on conflict, in the next several tips, we will address the various styles on our way to win/win. Today's style is Avoidance.

Avoidance: Research shows 25% of all conflicts at work get handled by avoidance. This is a lose/lose style. You can't resolve a conflict that hasn't been dealt with.

When you avoid something, where does it go? It goes inside.

And how do you know? Probably because you feel it like stress, headaches, hypertension, ulcers, pains in various parts of the body. There is a physiological response. It actually gets stuck in your body.

The pain also grows. Today you are irritated. Next week you're mad. Then next month you're enraged. Then comes blow up. In blow up, it is often difficult to trace back to the original event.

As I said above, this is a lose/lose construct. No one wins.

Next tip we'll discuss Cooperate or Collaborate--a win/win strategy.

If you have questions, comments, feedback, or topics you'd like covered, please continue to email me at rosanne@HumanTechTips.com.

Tip #57

Cooperate/Collaborate

Continuing our conversation on conflict, this tip is about win/win. Today's style is Cooperate or Collaborate.

Cooperate or collaborate: The idea here is that it's possible to have a conflict not me versus you, but you and I together facing the problem across from us. It is issue oriented, rather than people oriented. The focus is placed on the problem, concern or request, rather than the person on the other end of the line or across from you. How do you accomplish this?

One way is to neutralize the conversation. This means avoid using the pronoun 'you' or implying the customer caused the problem.

For example, 'you forgot to fax us' leaves no room for any other possibility than to put the blame on the customer. Perhaps someone in his or her office dropped the ball. The object is to get to a solution, not to assign responsibility.

In this instance, you could say 'the fax was not received,' or 'our records indicate blah blah blah.' This is called a no fault approach suggesting that perhaps an abstract third party may have forgotten to send the fax, rather than pointing a finger and making the customer wrong which, of course, gets you nowhere and turns into the win/lose construct.

Another neutral approach is to call an error to their attention by paraphrasing. For example: "Let me see if I have this right." often the person sees the error without prompting because they heard it said differently by another person, you, without your using any judgmental language.

Specifically this could show up around dates, where they think they told you the correct date but perhaps were doing two things at once and were mixed up. Rather than saying, "you don't mean that," or "those can’t be the right dates," repeat the dates that were given to you. In this way, the customer can hear their mistake and correct it, again without any blame or criticism.

If you have questions, comments, feedback, or topics you'd like covered, please continue to email me at rosanne@HumanTechTips.com.

Tip #58

European Customer Service

I've just returned from a European trip and want to report that customer service leaves a lot to be desired in two countries I visited.

However, while going through a souvenir shop at the Helsinki airport, I came across something I wanted to buy for my granddaughter. I wasn't sure what it was and asked, only to learn it was a zipper pull. It attaches to a zipper and has an animal or animated figure dangling from the end. Never having seen one before, I liked the idea of it. This was perfect and would easily fit into my luggage which was totally full.

But I wasn't familiar with what was dangling. Was it a bear? What was it?

The clerk told me it was a Moomin, and of course, I asked what that meant. She said it was a very popular animated figure (I assumed it was like Barney here in the States). While I was paying for it, another clerk brought a book over to me and invited me to look through it because it tells the story of the Moomins. They are very simpatico people, she said.

I was very impressed with what she did. First of all, she wasn't even the person waiting on me so she truly went the extra mile. Secondly, instead of just telling me, she went to the shelf and handed me a book and let me look through it. It was about US$25 so I wasn't interested in purchasing it, nor was she trying to sell it to me.

I read some, looked at the pictures, and skimmed through the book. When I found how empathetic the Moomins were, I told the clerk she was a "Human Moomin." She was beaming, smiling from ear to ear, and we all (including anyone in ear shot) had a good laugh.

I walked away feeling really good about Helsinki, good about myself, and I'm sure the clerks felt good about themselves too, truly win, win, win.

As you may recall in past tips, I used the word lagniappe--giving customers more than they expected. That certainly happened to me at the Helsinki Airport.

Where can you give your customers more than they expect?

If you have questions, comments, feedback, or topics you'd like covered, please continue to email me at rosanne@HumanTechTips.com.

Tip #59

Acknowledge/ Appreciate

Remember when you were a kid, or with your own kids, when they came home with the hand painting from school, and said, "Look what I made?" And you said, "Wow, that's terrific I'm going to put it on the refrigerator?" And then they made more and they were all on the refrigerator? Do you recall how exciting that was for each of you?

Then we get older and it's harder to acknowledge and appreciate each other, or our kids. For instance, let's say I'm new at your company and I have a report to do and I have 7 days to do it in. I do all the work. I stay late; I do the research. I put it together in great form. I don't sleep for days and I bring it to you two days ahead of schedule.

You are on the phone at the time and look up and see me and say, "Wow, give it to me. I need to get off the phone and look at this. This is really nice, Rosanne, very professional, very nicely thought out and laid out." And what do I say? "Oh, it was nothing." Right? Now if you were on the phone and I came in and you said 'Just leave it on the desk,' I would walk out and say something like, he or she is so ungrateful, I worked days and nights on this and brought it in early, etc. etc.

You work with most of your co-workers or peers day in and day out, some of you for years now through the good, the bad, and the ugly, not to mention Winter, Summer, Spring, and Fall. I invite you to authentically--not made up, not lip service-- but authentically, acknowledge or express appreciation for a co-worker, peer, direct report, manager, you choose the person. And then notice how you feel? Usually it's a pretty good feeling.

Remember this is not about getting something back, but rather, expressing something authentic for yourself.

Now if one of your co-workers also gets these tips and acknowledges you, be sure to take a deep breath and receive it.

Then notice which was easier to give the acknowledgment or receive it?

If you have questions, comments, feedback, or topics you'd like covered, please continue to email me at rosanne@HumanTechTips.com.

Tip #60

Employee Accountability

We find that in many organizations there is a parent-child relationship, rather than the manager or supervisor-employee relationship. With the former, it's hard to hold people responsible and accountable. Parent-child relationships at work are not only unprofessional and inappropriate, but are non productive and self defeating.

Let's take an instance where an employee is absent – beyond whatever you would consider normal. Besides the fact that they may have used up all their sick days, vacation days, etc. there is serious disruption to productivity. Morale gets depleted as other employees have to pick up the slack, and resentment often brews.

How do you handle this? Awareness is the first step. Make people aware of the impact and influence their attendance, or lack thereof, has on the total picture (and the bottom line).

What can you then do? Hold people accountable by having them replace themselves if they're going to be absent. Or, if someone wants to come in on a different shift, they should switch with someone else, thereby being responsible and accountable for their job.

This creates a win/win/win scenario. The employee gets what they want (by being pro-active in making the arrangements) and the other employees aren't negatively impacted, and then organizations have the proper personnel in place on a daily basis.

Make no mistake, attendance impacts productivity. The formula we presented in Tip #48 clearly reflects how inter-related attendance, adherence to schedule, and occupancy are, and the impact on productivity at your companies.

If you have questions, comments, feedback, or topics you'd like covered, please continue to email me at rosanne@HumanTechTips.com.

Tip #61

Impatience

In a previous tip, we charted customer's hold perceptions and learned that the longer they were on hold, the longer their perception was of being on hold.

Today's tip continues in this vein regarding customer's patience, or, I should say, impatience.

A research study done by Dimension Data shows that Americans are impatient when waiting in queue and are quicker to abandon calls than anywhere else in the world.

Americans are so impatient – they're willing to wait an average of only 37 seconds for their calls to be answered before they abandon the call.

However, the rest of the world exhibits greater patience:

Europe, the Middle East and Africa - willing to wait 67 seconds

Asia-Pacific customers are the most patient – willing to wait 72 seconds

What's your average queue time? Your Average Speed of Answer? (do you know?)

Here's some best practice statistics for you to compare yourself to.

Inbound Performance Metrics

BenchmarkPortal Report

	Average	Best Practices
80% Calls Answered (°)	36.7	18.3
ASA (° = seconds)	34.6	21.2
Average Talk Time (min)	6.1	3.3
Average After Call (min)	6.6	2.8
Average Calls Abandon (%)	5.5	3.65
Average Queue Time (°)	45.3	28.1
Average One/Done (%)	70.5	86.8
Average Calls/Shift	69.0	73.9
Attendance (%)	86.8	94.7

Where are you? Are corrections needed? My caveat regarding statistics: Use them as guidelines, not hard and fast rules.

Remember, people don't care what you know, until they know you care.

If you have questions, comments, feedback, or topics you'd like covered, please continue to email me at rosanne@HumanTechTips.com.

Tip #62

Email

One of the most difficult channels through which to serve customers is one of the simplest technologies to implement. Yes, it's email.

The challenge is less about technology and more about human factors and the staggering volume of queries

We all know that there are differences between written and verbal communications. Of course, verbal matters the most because you use the customer's name, and you use your voice inflection to communicate tone and mood.

However, tone and inflection are completely lost in email. Therefore, clarity is as important as sentence structure, grammar, and punctuation.

Effective summarizing and being brief are critical in email.

I see the human challenges as:

- Clarity – as I just mentioned
- Asynchronous nature of messaging

On the phone, you engage in a quick back and forth exchange and get to the root of the problem/issue/complaint. Having the same conversation via email takes more time and sometimes many more exchanges to reach resolution.

Tip: If the exchange goes on for a couple of days without coming to resolution, pick up the telephone and call the customer. It shows you are committed to resolving the issue in a timely fashion.

- Lack of immediacy

As you know, time can elapse between interactions. At the same time, some customers review their email only sporadically. So in a critical situation, email, and its lack of immediacy, is highly inefficient.

- Personal attention

Even in an email, have a salutation that includes the person's name, "Dear Mary," for instance. I hate emails that have no salutation at all. It feels sterile and rude to me.

In future tips we'll explore strategies for success, the various types of email responses, and email etiquette.

If you have questions, comments, feedback, or topics you'd like covered, please continue to email me at rosanne@HumanTechTips.com.

Tip #63

Email Strategies

Following are 4 simple strategies for success:

1) Respond quickly/promptly

2) Handle any request through the customer's choice of medium. If the customer emails you, respond via email. If the customer faxes you, fax back the customer. If the customer calls you on the telephone, phone the customer back.

3) Be brief and be clear...this reduces the back and forth of unnecessary correspondence.

4) Personalized service...this is still the caveat of the day.

Otherwise, you risk alienating the customer and ultimately losing them.

Tip: Combine automation with enough inspection or intervention to assure quality, consistency, and a personalized response.

Many companies use departmental or work group email addresses rather than individuals. This allows the group to monitor inbound activity, balance its distribution, and assess the quality.

No matter how you do it, the focus shouldn't be on the message but rather, on engaging the customer in a personalized fashion, regardless of the channel of communication used.

If you have questions, comments, feedback, or topics you'd like covered, please continue to email me at rosanne@HumanTechTips.com.

Tip #64

Email Organization

Organization of your email response:

Subject line - put the 'bottom line' in the subject line. What is the email all about? Put that in the subject line. If there are timelines, put those in the subject line or use an attention grabbing note, such as: deliverables by, or action required or requested by such and such a date.

Salutation - personalize. Dear first name.

Opening paragraph - rephrase the reason for the email. When you get an email that says, "thank you for taking the time to contact us", do you remember why you contacted them? I don't. Rather, put the reason such as "thank you for informing us of the difficulty you are experiencing with the installation of the CD program __________."

Next paragraph - your actual response

Closing paragraph – detailed description what action is to be or has been taken. Or, that this completes the inquiry, resolution, or your request has been fulfilled. A new CD is on its way to you via _______ and you should have it no later than ________.

Close - Sincerely, regards, and your name or at the least, your company

If you have questions, comments, feedback, or topics you'd like covered, please continue to email me at rosanne@HumanTechTips.com.

Tip #65

Email Responses

Basically, there are 3 types of responses:

- Automated
- Response with a template
- Response without template

And there are 3 R's of response:

- Receipt
- Response
- Resolution

Let's look at each. What are receipts?

- Automatic/instantaneous
- Confirmation of orders
- Acknowledgment of emails
- Sent prior to investigating, resolving, or fulfilling a request

Usually they are confirming or acknowledging the message. You may want to advise when they can expect a response.

Be sure to under commit and overperform. For instance, if you usually get back to people within 5 days, tell them 7-10 days. Then do get back to them in 5 days, and they'll be pleased (maybe even surprised). You also eliminate unnecessary emails or phone calls using this strategy. If you told me 5 days and it was the fifth day and I hadn't heard anything, what would I do (as a typical customer)? I'd email or call.

If you have questions, comments, feedback, or topics you'd like covered, please continue to email me at rosanne@HumanTechTips.com.

Tip #66

The 2nd "R"

The second R is Responses. They:

- Answer a question
- Update regarding an action you're taking, or has been taken
- Keep customers in the loop
- Provide timeframe for expected communication

What is common among each of these is to keep the customer advised. The communication tells them that you are working on the issue, that you have not forgotten about them.

Or in my case, if I do not hear from you, I think my request has fallen through the cracks.

We'll cover the third R - Resolution - next tip.

If you have questions, comments, feedback, or topics you'd like covered, please continue to email me at rosanne@HumanTechTips.com.

Tip #67

The 3rd "R"

The third R is Resolutions. They:

- Address the customer's request
- Thoroughly answer the question
- Solve/resolve the complaint or problem
- Satisfy the customer that this is complete

Ultimately, the resolution message's job is to satisfy the customer. And how do you know if you have accomplished this? Yes, you ask the customer.

If you have questions, comments, feedback, or topics you'd like covered, please continue to email me at rosanne@HumanTechTips.com.

Tip #68

Email Etiquette

Email Etiquette includes:

- A clear/concise subject line
- A personal salutation
- Spell out words/phrases/ jargon (use sparingly)
- Cohesiveness...smooth transitions/tone
- Commitments...what promises have you made?
- Spell-check/proofread/ grammar-check
- No capital letters (screaming)
- Closing

Tip: Complicated, complex, and/or controversial emails: Print them out prior to sending. Read then out loud, make any corrections, and then send. This simple step can save lots of misunderstandings.

Email is a fact of life today and it's becoming an increasingly comfortable means of communication. So it's inevitable that you will use email as a key channel. The challenge is to make it a tool that aids the customer and also ultimately benefits you and your company.

If you have questions, comments, feedback, or topics you'd like covered, please continue to email me at rosanne@HumanTechTips.com.

Tip #69

Verbal Patterns

Watch your verbal (as well as writing) patterns:

1) Don't ask a question that hides a statement, such as "Do you think that's a good idea?" This hides a statement. It would be better to say, "That seems ineffective or inefficient to me because..."

2) Watch yourself for tag questions. For instance, "It's cold in here, isn't it?" In this example, you are trying to get agreement and/or approval from someone other than yourself. The suggestion being that you don't have your own opinions. If you think it's cold, say so with a period at the end of the sentence, not a question mark. Avoid using tag questions.

3) Be on the lookout for disclaimers--prefaces to what we say. "It probably

isn't very important but," "I know I should know this but," "This is probably a silly idea but." What it actually says it 'Don't pay attention to what I'm about to say,' and so people don't. If you do ask a silly or stupid question, the other person will let you know. So leave our disclaimers.

4) Avoid frequent qualifiers such as probably, sort of, maybe. They take away strength from your message.

5) Interruptions. Aren't they irritating? Either you get interrupted or you interrupt. People interrupt for many reasons. One is what you are saying isn't as important as what I'm saying; I'm more important than you. However, If you don't stop it, you allow It. And it takes two people to allow an interruption.

The way out? "Excuse me, I wasn't quite finished" and keep going. Now let's say you've done this two times and now you can do what they do. Raise your voice and keep talking. One person backs down and it doesn't always have to be you.

The goal is powerful communications.

If you have questions, comments, feedback, or topics you'd like covered, please continue to email me at rosanne@HumanTechTips.com.

Tip #70

Questions

For instance, when asking questions:

- Only ask one question at a time. That's all the customer is going to answer.

- Ask the question that you are looking for a specific answer to. In other words, start at the end—what information will move this interaction to a successful conclusion in a timely fashion—then ask the appropriate question.

- Speak firmly and confidently. Don't ramble

- Wait until the person is done answering before jumping in. Don't step on their words. It usually has them either starting over or being frustrated with you.

- Don't assume you know where they're going. Let them take you there. Sometimes we think we know what they want, and in our earnestness to serve, we take them where we think they want to go--which is not where they wanted to go in the first place.

- Thank them for taking the time to call/write/fax, and then ask them if there is anything else you can help them with.

- Before you reply, ask them if there is anything else they'd like to add before you respond.

- Close the call by reiterating what action *they* or *you* are going to take, if any, to move the interaction to resolution.

If you have questions, comments, feedback, or topics you'd like covered, please continue to email me at rosanne@HumanTechTips.com.

Tip #71

Ask the Customer

In past tips I've said that if you want to know how you're doing in the area of customer service, ask the customer.

Taking it a step further, begin to use the customers' words. How do you find these out? Record customer calls from time to time and only listen for the language they use. This is not about anyone else at this point. You are focused on the customer's side of the conversation.

Why am I suggesting this? Because if you communicate with words that are familiar to the customer (1) you establish rapport more quickly, (2) you can move onto a productive resolution of whatever the interaction calls for, and (3) thus shorten the call, thereby (4) improving your bottom line.

Where would you use the customer's language?

- FAQs on your website
- Correspondence by email or snail mail
- Live conversations with customers, both internal and external

When customers think they're being understood, a connection is made. The last thing they expect is that you will understand them so they approach you somewhat hesitant and are pleasantly surprised that you're 'in synch with them,' 'on the same page,' words to that effect.

But don't take my word for it. Try it, track it, and notice the difference.

If you have questions, comments, feedback, or topics you'd like covered, please continue to email me at rosanne@HumanTechTips.com.

Tip #72

Thank You's

Let's say a customer calls with an upset. "I'm so upset, you were supposed to credit my account for $125.00, and instead you charged me $125.00!"

My suggestion is to respond with something like this: "Thank you so much for calling. I'm so sorry that happened to you. My name is Rosanne and together we're going to get to the bottom of this."

Sometimes you don't want to say 'thank you' but I promise you it makes a difference, It makes a difference not only to the customer, but to you as well. To the customer, that's the last thing they expect to hear. After all, who wants to say thank you to someone who is yelling at them. And it diffuses some of their upset because they now can be heard which is most of what they want anyway.

However, you do mean it because if they didn't call, you would not have the opportunity to turn them around, to take them to a productive interaction or resolution of their problem.

I'm sure you have all had the experience of an upset or irate customer calling and you made a difference, you listened, you empathized, and you assisted them in their plight. You turned the call around and made it a winner, and perhaps even took a customer beyond satisfied and to loyal.

So be authentic when you say "thank you so much for calling" (and giving me the opportunity to help you, win you back, solve your problem, or whatever).

If you have questions, comments, feedback, or topics you'd like covered, please continue to email me at rosanne@HumanTechTips.com.

Tip #73

S.P.A.C.E.

This tip is about 'stuff.'

You know how 'stuff' seems to accumulate?

We've got an acronym to help. It's called S.P.A.C.E.

S = sort
P = purge
A= assign a place
C = containerize
E = equalize

So what do we mean by this?

Sort means to put things in categories, like for like. The end goal is to store like with like but for now we're at sort to see what your 'stuff' consists of. A good place to begin is to clear the biggest space the fastest. So if you have a month's worth of newspapers all over a room, stack them neatly in a pile. I discard all but the last few days (after skimming headlines) because old News is just that: old!

I sort my mail by importance – some envelopes get tossed without even being opened, such as credit card offers.

- Sort loose papers into piles
- Put files into boxes
- Separate clothes by type and/or color

Next is Purge. What do you keep and what do you throw away, give away, or even. sell? Keep only things that build your energy, nourish your soul, and move your life forward. You might want to have three piles:

(1) Keep for sure
(2) "Maybe" and
(3) Give away, sell, or even throw away.

When "maybe" is still around after 30 days, it goes to the #3 spot.

Assign a place. Where will they go?

Containerize: What kind of container will you need to hold them?

Tip: Build up what you cannot spread out. For example, I get lots of industry publications, some monthly, some bi-weekly. I keep them all in one place, in one pile. When I travel, I take them with me, skim through most of them, and tear out important articles and then toss the magazines.

When I'm off the road, I take them home and read them while I'm watching TV (multi-tasking, of course).

Equalize. Stuff keeps coming in, like the mail and magazines. Bring only what you need into your workspace or house. And then keep it in a designated space.

Why? If there is lots of clutter in your personal and/or professional life, where's the space to be at choice, to be with the customer/co worker/friends/family, etc.? If you believe (like I do) that our external clutter represents our internal clutter, this is a good place to begin

If you have questions, comments, feedback, or topics you'd like covered, please continue to email me at rosanne@HumanTechTips.com.

Tip #74

Listening

Specifically, let's look at what prevents you from listening? For example:

Environmental distractions:

- You might be on the telephone with a customer when a coworker shoves a piece of paper in front of your face.
- You might notice how many customers are in queue.
- Third ear syndrome--tuned in to what is going on in the background. If this happens, it might be because: you care about your coworkers and customers.
- You overhear someone solving a tricky problem you spent a lot of time solving the previous day.

- You hear someone resolving a tricky problem you couldn't resolve.

Jumping ahead:

- You might be focusing on what you are going to say next.
- You mentally jump ahead in the conversation.

This has to do with two factors. First, you are expected to solve problems as quickly as possible.

Second, you can listen at a faster rate than you can speak.

Emotional filters:

Some of you serve the same customer base most of the time. Because of this, you may get to know some of your customers and develop an emotional response to them. These are called 'emotional filters.' For example, you might "brace yourself" whenever a particular customer calls. Avoid this. Keep an open mind from the beginning of every conversation.

Mental side trips:

Let's say it's 11:30 in the morning, and you get the type of call you've been handling all day long. You know what the customer is going to say; you've handled a number of these calls already. so you're wondering, "Where will I go for lunch?" You re-engage yourself in the conversation and find that you haven't lost too much. The customer continues to talk, and you work together to define the problem.

Maybe you think you know what the customer is going to say next, so you decide you're going to eat lunch at a certain restaurant because it's next door to a shop you'd like to visit. You start thinking about what you are going to buy, and so on. Now you're on a mental side trip. You come back into the conversation, but you've lost it. Your mental side trip has gone on for too long. You've wasted time, and you have to back track in the conversation by asking the customer to repeat what was said.

Being aware of this tendency will help you hang in with what the customer is saying.

Based upon good intentions, the above detract from your ability to focus on the task at hand, which is, of course, handling your current interaction, be it on the phone or face to face

If you have questions, comments, feedback, or topics you'd like covered, please continue to email me at rosanne@HumanTechTips.com.

Tip #75

Effective Listeners

- Accomplish results more timely
- Get the right information from the get go
- Reduce the margin of error
- Focus on what the customer is saying (instead of what you're going to be saying next)
- Build rapport (based on genuine interest and caring)

How does the above get accomplished?

The first step is being present to the customer--not in the past or the future or the next transaction. We all know when we have been listened to, and especially when someone is only giving is 30%. Give 100%.

We'll have an acronym for you next tip.

If you have questions, comments, feedback, or topics you'd like covered, please continue to email me at rosanne@HumanTechTips.com.

Tip #76

L.A.R.C.

Here's an easy acronym to remember:

L isten -- listen to what the customer is and is not saying; what do you hear behind the words (upset, anger, frustration, fear?)

A cknowledge - acknowledge what you hear, i.e., if I understand you, here's what happened and here's what you would like us to do for you.

R espond - respond appropriately.

C lose - close the call with thanking the person for contacting you, and asking if there is anything else you can do for them. You also may want to repeat any action that either you or they need to take on the matter discussed.

If you have questions, comments, feedback, or topics you'd like covered, please continue to email me at rosanne@HumanTechTips.com.

Tip #77

Do’s and Don’ts

Do:

- Listen

  Tell the customer what you can do (here's what I can do in this instance)

- I'll find out and get back to you (and do)

- Cement what you can or will do

Don't:

- Interrupt (let the customer finish what they are saying)

- Say "I can't" (rather here's what I can do)

- Say "I don't know" (rather I'll find out)
- Start a sentence with 'no'

If you have questions, comments, feedback, or topics you'd like covered, please continue to email me at rosanne@HumanTechTips.com.

About the Author

Rosanne D'Ausilio, Ph.D., an industrial psychologist, consultant, master trainer, best selling author, executive coach, customer service expert, and President of Human Technologies Global, specializes in human performance management. Over the last nearly 25 years, she has provided needs analyses, instructional design, and customized, live customer service skills trainings as well as executive/leadership coaching.

Known as 'the practical champion of the *human,'* she authors 14 best sellers "*Wake Up Your Call Center: Humanize Your Interaction Hub,"* 4th ed, "*Customer Service and the Human Experience,"* "Lay Your Cards on the Table: 52 Ways to Stack Your Personal Deck (includes

32-card deck of cards)—motivational and inspirational readings, *How to Kick Your Customer Service Up A Notch: 101 Insider Tips,* Volume I and II, The Expert's Guide to Customer Service, Volume I and II, Kindle editions and Create Space Series, as well as her popular, complimentary 'tips' newsletter on *How To Kick Your Customer Service Up A Notch*! at http://www.HumanTechTips.com

She represents the *human* element on the Advisory Board of an Italian software company, authors numerous articles for industry newsletters, and is a much sought after dynamic, vibrant, internationally prominent keynote speaker.

She can be reached at Rosanne@human-technologies.com

www.ingramcontent.com/pod-product-compliance
Lightning Source LLC
LaVergne TN
LVHW010116170826
845678LV00012B/2439